T0199135

My Chocolate

BUTTERFLY

Reflections on a Bike Trip from
Lake Oswego, Oregon to Oswego, New York

ANN C. MULVANY CARON
on behalf of
Dr. Paul Caron in Heaven

WestBow Press books may be ordered through booksellers or by contacting:

WestBow Press
A Division of Thomas Nelson & Zondervan
1663 Liberty Drive
Bloomington, IN 47403
www.westbowpress.com
844-714-3454

ISBN: 978-1-6642-7224-8 (sc)
ISBN: 978-1-6642-7225-5 (e)

Library of Congress Control Number: 2022912769

Print information available on the last page.

WestBow Press rev. date: 03/07/2024

WESTBOW
PRESS®
A DIVISION OF THOMAS NELSON
& ZONDERVAN

My Chocolate
BUTTERFLY

Dedication

To Dr. Paul Caron,
my loving and fun husband of 17 years,
whom I had the honor and privilege of knowing for over 22 years,
who was a great Dad to sons Matt and Adrian,
and
who dedicated his life to making a positive impact
on youth and student-athletes of all ages
in his roles as teacher, professor, and coach to many.
I will forever love you and miss you.
Hopefully, I made you proud in you becoming
a published author from Heaven!

12/3/1946 - 1/30/2017

Acknowledgments

The original text was written by my husband Dr. Paul Caron in 1994. It was published in Oswego County Business Magazine in its August/September edition and was the basis for how we met during a chance encounter at a groundbreaking ceremony at Alcan Aluminum in Oswego, New York in the Fall 1994. Paul served as the Director of the Greater Oswego Chamber of Commerce at that time and had returned from his cross- country bike trip from Lake Oswego, Oregon to Oswego, New York – a trip that spanned 45 days and approximately 3,000 miles. I was the Recycling Coordinator for Oswego County's Division of Solid Waste and coincidentally had just returned from a National Recycling Coalition Conference that was held in Portland, Oregon.

The Journey From Lost to Found

When you start a ride like this that takes you over so many of the United States, where you meet so many different and amazing people, various thoughts sort of jog through your mind that come from the past. And for about 45 days and approximately 3,000 miles covering 13 states, I have had some wonderful moments where my reflections have been rich and rewarding.

The Downhill Chase and Reflections of a Simpler Time

It was actually the second or third day of the trip, when I first came on to Mount Hood, Oregon, and into a fairly heavy snowstorm. I was racing rapidly down the hill. It must have been the speed of the downhill chase that took me back to a moment when my life was much simpler. As a young man around 12 or 13, my life – like that of many people my age – was taken up by Ted Williams, blueberry pie, my grandmother's store, fresh homemade bread, winking at girls, worrying about my report card, and the dread of having to go to dance school when it wasn't really macho back then. So, as I raced down Mount Hood, I felt invulnerable. It reminded me of how proud I was as a kid, maybe because life was so neat back then.

A Winning Baseball Game

I remembered a baseball game that took place years ago. I was the playground leader at Forest River Park in Salem, Massachusetts on the North Shore of Boston, and had to pull all the guys together and pick the teams. You know, you threw the bat up in the air and put your fingers up and down the bat to pick the teams. Back then you tried not to be mean to people. You picked the best team you could, even though we were just kids and fairly innocent. Even then I wanted to win.

An Oversized Hershey's Bar, A Louisville Slugger and An Unexpected Butterfly Encounter

That particular day, our team won, and I had a wonderful day. I must have hit a couple of home runs, and I was very proud. My chest was swollen as I rounded the bases perhaps the second or third time. And even though I was very young, I really thought life was pretty cool and pretty easy, and actually pretty basic. I might have been outgrowing that period in my life, but I walked home very proud of what I had achieved that day. I was getting a bit smug and egotistical about my achievements. After the game, I stopped at my grandmother's store, and left with my glove in one hand and a huge, oversized Hershey bar in the other.

Healing An Injured Soul

It was a hot day, so the Hershey Bar was melting. Draped over my shoulder was my favorite Louisville Slugger. As I strolled home, something landed on my shoulder and kept buzzing by my ear. I wasn't sure what it was, and it wouldn't go away. It was annoying me as I was reflecting on all of my great achievements. Finally, it annoyed me so much that I looked to see what it was. It appeared to be just a nuisance butterfly. In my wildest dreams, I never thought I could swipe my bat at it and hit it. However, I had had a good day so I thought I'd give it a try. I spontaneously swung my bat – my Hershey bar sitting in my other hand – and to my amazement and conquest, I struck that butterfly. I watched it roll wing over wing and swirl to the ground. Then it struck me that I didn't want to be so successful, I didn't want to be the great hitter – I didn't want to hurt that butterfly, so I grabbed for it with my glove and the butterfly landed in my mitt and got all gooped up with chocolate. Without knowing what to do, I dropped everything – the bat, the glove, the Hershey bar and the butterfly who was just trying to be a friend. I then realized that the butterfly was beautiful, and it wasn't hurting anyone. It was just what it was – a beautiful, beautiful butterfly. I took that butterfly, carefully covered it with my other hand, threw the Hershey bar away, and put the bat under my arm. I walked home because I wanted to see if I could save my new friend.

Fly, Rise and Soar

Well, my Mom helped me as we delicately took an eyedropper to rinse the chocolate off its wings with the hope that it would again fly. After a half hour or so, the butterfly darted off of the kitchen sink and out the little window. And I was sad that day because I had injured a friend and it was a simple friend, with simple values. And it was *my chocolate butterfly*.

Everyone Playing Their Part, Everyone Caring

As I reflect on my flight down Mount Hood, I wonder why our lives can't be as simple as that butterfly. My new friendship with that new butterfly was based on <u>mutual respect</u>. I thought of that as I dashed down Mount Hood at 42 miles an hour. This bike ride was all about pride. It was about simple things, nothing complicated. It wasn't political. It was about good people with good values — that's what pride is. It's not about trading away truth for some future favor. Pride is *everyone* — everyone in the community, <u>every single person</u> in the community *caring*.

Owning Your Part

I'd like to see the streets clean. I'd like to see flowerpots everywhere. I'd like to see merchants with their stores open extra hours – evenings and weekends. I'd like to see adults stop kids when they litter. I'd like to see adults stop kids when they swear, or women correct men when they are rude or sexist. Pride is having the nicest ball parks in the community, the cleanest, sharpest, best schools, and the best teachers. Pride really has no particular boundaries. It's what you want it to be. And yet we seem to accept the average when it comes to our community. You know, it's easy to play it safe, it's easy to criticize, but it's not so easy to stand up and be counted – to own your part in being responsible and accountable. This trip is about standing up and being counted.

Working Together

I'm concerned with the posturing of decision makers. I don't like to "get along, one must go along." It's pretty simple to me, if we agree on it, let's go do it, and share in the enjoyment of doing it. Pride is participating, not asking if you can, not waiting for an engraved invitation. If something needs to be improved, you just do it and walk away from it without caring who gets the credit for it. But, you are proud because you've contributed.

Striving to Be Better

We have such tremendous resources in our community, a community so close to excellence. Let's not be satisfied. Let's not accept our community as it is now. Let's make it a whole lot better. Let's be as hospitable as the folks in Lake Oswego, Oregon. Let's try to find more friendly merchants, like the ones I ran into in Whitefish, Montana or the Native American from Oswego, Montana who literally gave me the hat off his head when I told him I was from Oswego, New York. Or the youth coordinator who went out of his way to let us join his kids in Fergus Falls, Minnesota. Or the absolutely spotless community of Richland Center, Wisconsin – they're proud. And I'm proud, and not going to compromise or trade away that pride. And I'm not going to worry about acceptance or popularity. As I see it, sometimes there will be consensus, sometimes there won't, but I don't worry about that. Deep down inside I really, truly believe that each of us must do our best and ask others to do likewise. To be the best community, the best chamber, the best individual. Pride comes from your childhood. It comes from being polite and courteous. Pride is feeling your heartbeat rapidly when you hear the National Anthem. Be proud when you make a difficult decision and stick by it through tough times.

Taking A Chance

I wish every person in our community could recall a story like "My Chocolate Butterfly" and maybe that will stretch each of us to be our best. That comes from being proud, it comes from taking chances, it comes from having a vision, not from critical, judgmental, divisive rhetoric. I would challenge anyone who reads this and wants to make our community better, to seek me out so that we can work together. I challenge those who want to leave a better place for those who follow, to stop talking, put on your sneakers, roll up your sleeves, and do something.

Your Own Chocolate Butterfly

Don't wait to be invited. I'm proud of this trip and I'm proud of Oswego, but we've got a long way to go. "My Chocolate Butterfly" is going to guide me – I hope that each of you have your own "Chocolate Butterfly."

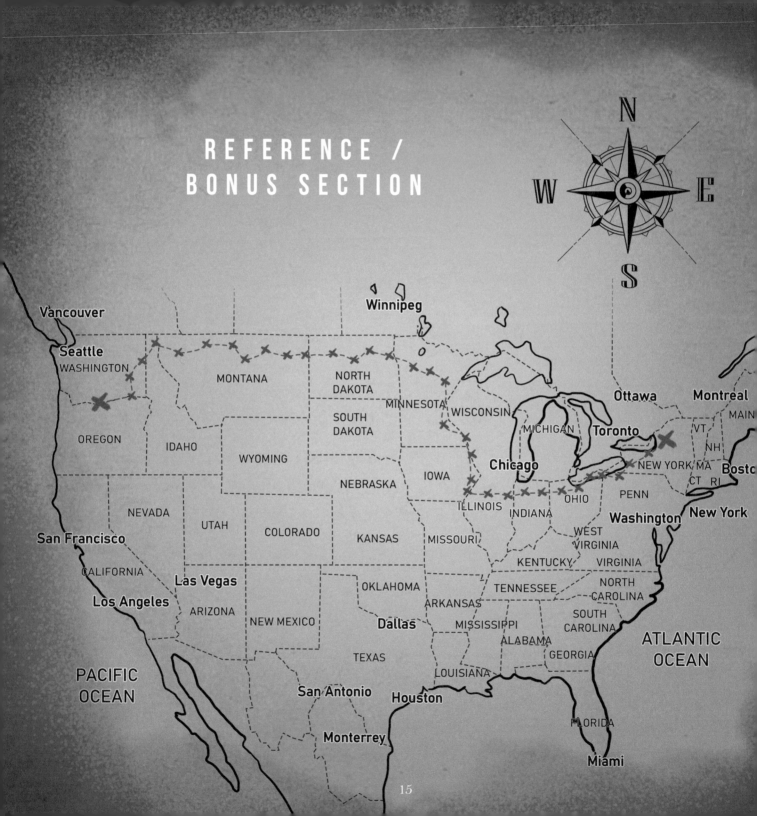

REFERENCE /
BONUS SECTION

List of Stops on the "Bike Ride for Pride" – 1994

	Depart	Arrive
• June 6	Lake Oswego	to Biggs, Oregon
• June 7		to Umatilla, Oregon
• June 8		to Lind, Washington
• June 9		to Spokane, Washington
• June 10		to Bonner's Ferry, Idaho
• June 11		to Kalispell, Montana
• June 13		to Browning, Montana
• June 14		to Chester, Montana
• June 15		to Havre, Montana
• June 16		to Malta, Montana
• June 17		to Wolf Point, Montana
• June 18		to Bainville, Montana
• June 20		to Stanley, Montana
• June 21		to Minot, North Dakota
• June 22		to Knox, North Dakota
• June 23		to Grand Forks, North Dakota
• June 24		to Bagley, Minnesota
• June 25		to Bemidji, Minnesota
• June 27		to Grand Rapids, Minnesota
• June 28		to Onamia, Minnesota
• June 29		to St. Paul, Minnesota
• June 30		to Winona, Minnesota
• July 1		to McGregor, Iowa
• July 2		to Maquoketa, Iowa

- July 4   to Muscatine, Iowa
- July 5   to Princeton, Illinois
- July 6   to Ottawa, Illinois
- July 7   to Chicago Heights, Illinois
- July 8   to Plymouth, Indiana
- July 9   to Fort Wayne, Indiana
- July 11   to Defiance, Ohio
- July 12   to Freemont, Ohio
- July 13   to Lorain, Ohio
- July 14   to Geneva, Ohio
- July 15   to Erie, Pennsylvania
- July 16   to Dunkirk, New York
- July 18   to Amherst, New York
- July 19   to Rochester, New York
- July 20   to Oswego, New York

Paul's Highly Recommended Books

- <u>All I Really Need To Know I Learned In Kindergarten</u> – Robert Fulghum
- <u>Don't Sweat The Small Stuff...and It's All Small Stuff</u> – Richard Carlson, Ph.D.
- <u>The Last Lecture</u> – Randy Pausch and Jeffrey Zaslow
- <u>The Science of Hitting</u> – Ted Williams and John Underwood
- <u>Have A Little Faith</u> – Mitch Albom

Printed in the United States
by Baker & Taylor Publisher Services